UNBAR

[uhn-bahr]

verb

To remove the bars from (a gate or door); unlock;
unbolt: "she unbarred the gate."

UNBAR

Rune Østgård & Mattis Storhaug

und
oqo

©2023 UNDOQO AS
undoqo.com

ISBN: 9798865576136

Author: Rune Østgård
Editor: Mattis Storhaug

Cover art: Mattis Storhaug
Illustrations: Mattis Storhaug
Typesetting: Mattis Storhaug

UNBAR makes a concise yet powerful case for supporting decentralized money, and explains why it is conducive to human flourishing in all its myriad forms.

– Lyn Alden, *Author of Broken Money*

UNBAR takes as its starting point some of the insights that Rune got when writing

Fraudcoin
– *1000 Years of Inflation as a Policy* and while he was preparing our next book,

Arrow of Truth
– *from Forseti to Satoshi and Beyond.*

An **open** mind is like a fortress with its gates unbarred and unguarded.

– Warhammer 40,000 Dawn of War

Some 20 years ago, I realized that I had spent 18 years in schools and universities without learning anything about our monetary system and the politics of money.

They hadn't even taught us how money is created.

I said to myself:

How can I expect to understand anything about politics and society if I don't understand money? – I must be blind as a bat.

– *Rune*

Preface

The year is 1720 and you are a Norwegian serf. In the mornings and the evenings, you till a small parcel of land that the king lets you use so you can feed your family. During daytime all of you must work for no pay on one of the king's many estates. It has been the same for generations.

One evening you come home and discover a bidding stick on your front door. The door has many marks from other sticks having been rammed into the wood. They always carry the same message – show up at the town square ready for war, if not you will be punished by death.

This time, it's different.

The sticks use to be blue. But this one is dark red.

You stare at the bidding stick a few seconds before you grab it and thug it out, leaving a fresh new mark in the wood.

Your body trembles as you uncork it.

You take out a piece of hide inscribed with the following text...

There is a weapon that is so powerful, that the one that controls it rules the rest of the world.

This weapon is directed at us, the people, continuously and it's the sole reason for our misery.

Our group have identified the weapon. We know where it is and how to destroy it.

Once we achieve our goal, we can all become free and prosperous.

We need your help to succeed.

Pass on the stick to your neighbor and meet us by the river at midnight.

If you fail to do this, you and your descendants will remain serfs forever!

— *The Rebels*

Now tell me...
– what do **you** do?

UNBAR helps you to free yourself from an intellectual prison.

A prison that has plagued us since rulers learned how to exploit the most powerful weapon:

The exorbitant privilege of creating money out of **nothing.**

Introduction

The dream that came true

The Wright brothers were bicycle mechanics who had dreamed of flying since they were young boys. Physics professors said it would be impossible, but Wilbur and Orville didn't care. They were curious about science and had been raised to be free thinkers. Optimism, trial and error were their method.

On 14 December 1903, in Kitty Hawk, North Carolina, they flipped coins about who should be the first to test their plane, the Flyer I. Wilbur won the toss, but his attempt was unsuccessful. On 17 December Orville managed to keep the airplane in the air for 12 seconds and cover a distance of 36.5 meters. They wrote history, and "the experts" had to eat humble pie.

Waking up

Now, imagine that you live in a remote area somewhere in the US at that time, but that you never have heard about people trying to fly in machines before. You're out walking and suddenly, out of the clouds, comes a giant metal bird roaring towards you. As it passes you get a glimpse of a man who waves at you.

How do you think your brain handles the fact that your eyes for the first time see a man flying in the sky? How long do you think it takes before your brain accepts what you just saw?

The fact of the matter is that you will in the end believe what you saw, and that you even will be comfortable with it. Later, most people will go through the same mental exercise. This is how the brain works. This is how we as human beings deal with discoveries.

When it comes to negative revelations, it's not as easy. But the process is the same. And if you know for a fact that a reward awaits you, it will be easier for you to deal with it.

Which brings us to the topic of the day:

Humankind has lived in two different forms of civilizations, one which is governed by the principle of **monetary freedom,** where people freely can use the money that they like best; and one which is governed by the principle that a ruler has a **monopoly on money creation**.

These two distinct forms of civilizations rest on very different belief systems and have produced vastly different outcomes.

Whether you have a PhD or only have done elementary school, it's a 99.99% certainty that you haven't been taught this.

Not understanding money and how different monetary systems affect society is like having your brain locked into a prison. You should take comfort in the fact that it's the same for almost everybody.

If you touch the key to unlock the insight into the consequences of what I just told you, your brain's emotional center will soon start screaming at you.

You see, no brain likes to be told that its software is invalid, that it has been unable to see the truth and that it instead has been exposed to a world of lies.

Especially your brain is going to protest wildly when it understands that a fraction of the people, a small group of elites, has had this insight, and that they have exploited you and your ancestors for generations.

Mayer Amstel Rothschild, the founder of the Rothschild finance dynasty, was one of the privileged few who knew this secret. He is purported to have said:

> *Give me control of a nation's money supply, and I care not who makes its laws.*

Rothschild probably meant that the one who controls the monetary system has so much power that he will be the one that rules a nation and its people.

Monetary freedom was civilizations' governing principle

Let us dig a little deeper into the matter, and look at something which is a lot more positive:

» The first civilizations that we have significant knowledge of emerged 5000 years ago.

» The principle of monetary freedom probably governed many civilizations for about 2500 years before the first rulers secured themselves a monopoly on money creation.

» The Norwegian region *Trøndelag* was one of the very last civilized parts of the West that managed to protect this core principle. It lasted exactly until the year 1050 AD.

» Rebels reintroduced the principle of monetary freedom in the Netherlands sometime after their uprising against the Habsburg empire in 1566. It gave them the Golden Age, as the new nation became one of the wealthiest and freest countries in the world, a position it kept for almost 150 years.

» Rebels once more introduced monetary freedom as a de facto governing principle in the US after their victorious revolution against the English in 1783. They picked up where the Dutch had started, and the US soon was to enjoy the status as the freest country in the world. It delivered a marvelous level of prosperity that pulled poor people out of poverty at a rate that humankind has never seen.

» The de facto principle of monetary freedom in the US lasted until the Coinage Act of 1857 removed the legal tender status for foreign coins.

Looking back, we see that monetary freedom has been the governing principle for most of the time when we have had civilizations. Furthermore, we see that it lasted for perhaps as much as about 300 years after it was rediscovered by the Dutch.

An idea can be put to sleep, but it can never be killed. The idea of monetary freedom has been dormant for 166 years.

It's about time to wake it up.

The threat of globalism

Historians who don't understand money are not historians.

Economists who don't understand history are not economists.

Politicians who understand neither money nor history are destined to make catastrophic errors.

And these three groups have in common that they are unable to predict the future with any degree of certainty.

Only those who have a good understanding of both money and history can make meaningful predictions about the future of our civilization.

And only those who have this knowledge can give sound advice about how the future should be shaped.

During the past 100 years we have seen enormous geopolitical changes, with a transition from a multi-polar order which ended in 1945, to a bipolar system that lasted until the implosion of the Soviet Union and the East Bloc in 1991, and to the unipolar US hegemony that we have had for a total of 32 years.

The question is – what comes next?

Lately we have been fed a narrative that dictates that a borderless hegemony dominated by global elites is inevitable, necessary and to the best for humanity.

Global challenges require global solutions

– they keep repeating to us.

Intellectuals, billionaires and political leaders have invested a lot of financial and political capital in this vision. Their idea is that we should set up a new world order, administered by the United Nations (UN) with the World Economic Forum (WEF) as an adviser.

The organizations are open about their grand idea. The WEF's website tells us:

We must work together to build a new world order

In 2019 the UN and the WEF signed an agreement for a strategic partnership. The stated goal was:

> *to accelerate the implementation of the UN's 2030 Agenda for Sustainable Development.*

UN Secretary-General António Guterres announced the agreement and said:

> *The new Strategic Partnership Framework between the United Nations and the World Economic Forum has great potential to advance our efforts on key global challenges and opportunities, from climate change, health and education to gender equality, digital cooperation*

and financing for sustainable development. Rooted in UN norms and values, the Framework underscores the invaluable role of the private sector in this work – and points the way toward action to generate shared prosperity on a healthy planet while leaving no one behind.

Although most of the Western countries have aligned themselves with these policy objectives for more than a decade, the people seem to be asleep.

The UN and the WEF want the world to be governed by their own supranational organizations, consisting of unelected people, working together with mega-corporations in a global, centrally planned economy. This is what we call "corporatism," which is the economic system of the political ideology known as fascism.

Those who raise their voices in protest have been "shot down" with slur, as globalists and oblivious citizens shout "conspiracy theorists" at them. As Elon Musk, the owner of *Tesla* and *X* has noted, it seems like many of the conspiracy theories have come true, something which the "Twitter files" clearly demonstrate. This means that the effect of the globalists' smearing weakens and that the number of people who ask questions and protest keep growing.

Wake up your inner rebel

I hold a view of the next phase in the development of civilization that is very different from the proponents of globalism.

I believe we have reached a peak state of centralization of political power, and that we will revert to a more decentralized society with a multipolar world order.

How fast this development will go – well that's a completely different question.

The reason why I believe this, is first of all that history proves that we the people can shape our own future.

It's always a small minority that leads the way. And we should aim at being part of this group that changes things for the better.

Furthermore, I know more about how the monetary system shapes civilization and politics than the intellectuals and communicators who fuel the revolutionary flame of the globalist elite.

And now I'm passing this knowledge on to you.

The battle of ideas

Monetary systems and monetary policies have a far bigger impact on how civilizations develop and on the changing geopolitical world order than most people understand.

Therefore, it's important that you have an in-depth knowledge of money if you want to interpret the past and understand the contemporary situation. If you lack these skills, trying to look into the future – or to change its course in a positive way – becomes a hopeless endeavor.

Professor Yuval Harari is a historian and philosopher by education. He has become quite influential in the WEF circles. The professor has written the international bestseller *Sapiens – A Brief History of Humankind,* published in 2015. The book has inspired many educated people to support a transition from today's unipolar world order to a borderless society ruled by intellectuals, bureaucrats and the super wealthy.

Harari's problem is that the book builds on an understanding of the monetary system which in my opinion is fatally flawed. As a result, the people who listen to him build their beliefs and hopes on outright false assumptions.

Central planning of the global population and our institutions on such a scale as the UN and the WEF plan to implement are bound to create an extreme amount of friction and human cost. This is why I let this book shed light on some of Harari's popular ideas.

You see – winning the battle of the ideas is of fundamental importance.

An outline of UNBAR

In the next chapter, I'll explain what money is. You will learn the most important lesson of them all, that a ruling class that controls "the money printer" always can use newly created money to crush dissent and keep popular resistance at a controllable level.

In the third chapter I'll show you how civilization scales in layers, in somewhat similar way as Rotschild argued. Here I will provide an analysis of how monetary systems have shaped the course of history.

But we will dive deeper into the analysis and look at how different types of monetary systems are layered upon very different types of *belief systems*.

I demonstrate how these belief systems have guided the monetary policies and how the monetary systems have shaped the global world order that we have today.

In the fourth chapter I'm going to discuss factors that threaten today's dominant monetary system, and by extension the American empire.

And finally, in chapter five, I'll shed light on the X-factor – *the distribution of knowledge about the monetary system*, and why it possibly is a catalyst that in combination with a handful of other factors will force the development of the world order and our civilization into a more positive direction.

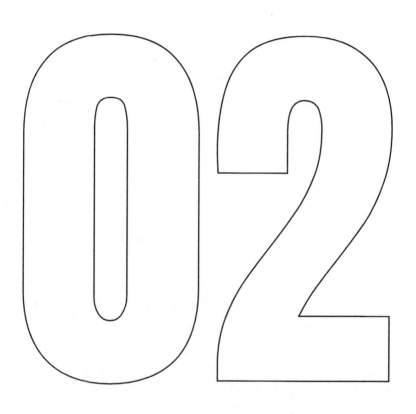

Money

Commodity money in a natural state

Money is properly defined as *a universal means of exchange*, meaning that you can use it to buy "everything." It's a concept that emerges naturally in society due to voluntary human interaction between people in what we call *the generous tit for tat game.*

Here's how it works:

Let's say that I don't know you and that I suddenly meet you in the desert. I have food, but I'm thirsty, and I don't have any water. You have water, but you're hungry, and you don't have any food.

We have many alternative actions we can choose between.

> We can avoid contacting each other.

> We can try to communicate with each other.

> Or we can try to attack each other and steal what the other one has.

We might try the peaceful solution and see if it's possible to cooperate. I start out by greeting you respectfully. When you return the favor, I might tell you where I'm from and where I'm heading. If the small talk runs smoothly, I might ask you if I can help you with something.

If we are successful with our little back and forth, we end up sharing the food and the water. In this way we can satisfy the needs of both parties. We might even agree to meet somewhere later, to see if we can continue to enjoy our little game.

This is the generous tit for tat. You probably realize by now that you know this game very well because you play it every day.

It's of fundamental importance to us as human beings. We need to play it, otherwise we won't be able to socialize at all.

As long as we both benefit from playing it, we might take it a little further. But if the favor isn't returned, we just break it off and go separate ways.

Let's return to the desert and tweak the situation a little bit.

You don't have enough water for the both of us, and you aren't hungry. But you have two camels, and if I can exchange something with you for one of them, then I can possibly make it to the nearest oasis and manage to survive.

I have some glass pearls that my people use as gifts and a means of exchange, but you come from a different culture, and unfortunately you don't see any value in them. I don't have anything else that you are interested in either. We're in a situation where we find ourselves unable to trade. The attempt to cooperate fails, and the question arises: Should I attack you, or hope that I find some luck later if I let you go?

The emergence of more commonly used means of exchange makes it more likely that we can succeed in cooperating with each other. It increases our options and reduces the risk of bloody outcomes.

As humans' ability to cooperate improves over time, the money also helps us to build capital together, and slowly a society that we call *civilization* emerges. With no money, we won't be able to build much capital as people are unable to develop advanced individual crafts and other skills. Without capital and what the economists call "the division of labor" we won't have any civilization.

Money is basically the cornerstone of civilization.

But how does something become money?

The answer is that some goods will be more popular than others. When many people want them, then it's easier to use them as a medium of exchange.

It's an advantage if the commodities have an intrinsic value, meaning that they are highly sought after due to qualities that make them useful or desirable. Durability, scarcity, divisibility and transportability matters too.

Animal hides, cocoa beans, tobacco leaves, pearls and shells have been used as money, but because they lacked one or more of these qualities, they lost the competition.

The "winners" were silver and gold.

The high degree of scarcity of these metals, especially of gold, is very important, because it ensures that the value will be relatively stable compared to the value of other commodities. If we use something as money that we easily can make more of, such as glass pearls, then the value of the money may fluctuate wildly.

In short, gold and silver had the qualities that enabled these metals to become universal means of exchange, typically in the shape of standardized coins. They became globally accepted money in a Darwinian-like process of natural selection.

Debt money in a natural state

Historically money has also emerged due to the use of debt.

I might not have something that I can pay you with today, but you trust that I will pay you tomorrow. You ask me if you can sell your claim on me to a third party, which I might agree to. In this way, debt and bills that provide proof of debt might begin to circulate as means of exchange.

Paper bills are easy to carry, making it possible to transport wealth over long distances. Some types of bills might become so popular that they end up being used as money in parallel with commodity money.

The drawback with debt as money is counterparty risk. You can never know for sure if the debtor will be willing and able to pay. In contrast with gold and silver coins, it becomes a game of trust, as the final settlement is being postponed.

Money in a political state

As we saw above, we can always choose between voluntary cooperation and violence.

Some people might be natural traders, while others might be naturally inclined to use coercion.

If a political society forms, a ruler will often be tempted to monopolize money creation. This enables the ruler to become *a legal counterfeiter* who can create money that he gives a privileged status, for instance by deciding that only his money can be used to pay taxes. In this way he coerces others to work to get access to the money that he creates.

This is the situation we have all over the world today. Based on a typical corporatist private-public partnership, the governments let the banking sector create new money when they issue loans.

A central bank co-ordinates how rapidly the private banks are allowed to create new money by setting a **"key interest rate."**

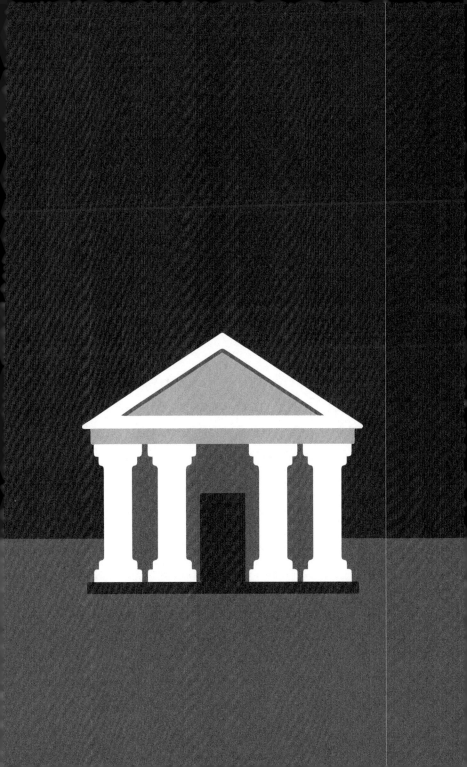

The central bank also buys the government's debt in the secondary market by creating new money. By doing this it makes it possible for the government to spend more money than it gets from taxation.

This privilege comes at a price. But it's not paid by the ruler.

The price is paid by those who receive the newly created money late, or who never receive it. They only see the effects of the money creation – rising prices.

Thus, as prices go up faster than their earnings, they must work harder to maintain their living standards.

In this way, wealth is transferred from workers and savers to the first recipients of the steady stream of newly created money.

This observation of how monetary policy extracts and transfers wealth is called *the Cantillon effect.*

Richard Cantillon was a French-Irish successful banker and one of the first classic economists. He observed these mechanisms firsthand when the fraudulent John Law created the famous Mississippi bubble in France in the early 18th century.

The observation shouldn't come as a surprise to anyone. If you are a counterfeiter, you will be the one who benefit the most. The first recipients of the money also benefit from the increased demand that your money represents.

Most people will be at a loss as the counterfeited money dilutes the value of the total stock of money, just like your lemonade tastes less when you pour water into it.

It's always the government and the wealthiest of the wealthy that benefit from monetary policy.

Today, those who become rich due to positioning themselves near the source where the new money is created are often referred to as *Cantillonaires*.

As time passes and the policy of inflation does its job, the middle class gets crushed by political money, while the poor is unable to climb the social ladder.

In a developed country, close to 100% of the total stock of money is created by debt.

This means, that if you shall participate in the competition to be the first receiver of new money, you must take out loans. And this is also what people do. They take out large loans and over time they become dependent on the banks.

Over time we, the people, become serfs who are beholden to two masters: A government that flees us through taxation and banks that collect interest payments from us on money that they have created out of nothingness.

There are four reasons why the super wealthy and the government always win the competition of getting hold of the most debt money:

Firstly

they are the ones that can post the most valuable collateral, meaning that they get the lowest interest rate, which again means that they can afford servicing more debt.

Secondly

they make sure that they aren't personally responsible for paying back the loans.

Thirdly

they are experts in rolling over their loans, ensuring that they always get hold of new and cheap loans that they can use to pay back their old loans with.

And fourthly

they invest the money they borrow, not only in consumer goods such as cars and homes like most people do, but also in capital that enables them to earn a profit.

The way a system based on political money is structured, explains among other things why

» even the gigantic Coca-Cola corporation relies on debt for financing its everyday operations

» Norwegian households, despite having among the highest average per capita income and typically two working adults, have the highest debt to income ratio in the world

» total global debt increased with 70% to a total of 300 T (trillion) USD after the money printing during the Covid-19 pandemic

We know from experience that everybody wants to get their hands on the new money.

And we see daily that the way to get it is to borrow from the banks.

The only problem is that we, the people, borrow money to become poor and subservient, while the super wealthy and the state borrow money to accumulate more wealth and political power.

Preliminary summary of the socio-economic concept of money

Money is properly defined as the universal means of exchange. It emerges naturally in society, in a Darwinian-like selection process. This is what we can call natural money.

As the quality of means of exchange improves, people can cooperate, build capital together, develop new skills and specialize, and develop a society based on the division of labor. We partly use money where we can have immediate settlement, typically coins of valuable metal, in addition to debt money, typically pieces of paper or as digitally inscribed numbers in ledgers maintained by computer networks controlled by banks.

People who are inclined to use force prefer to counterfeit money and coerce others to use their money and to work for them. This is what economists often refer to as "fiat money," but I prefer to use the term "political money." The transfer of wealth that occurs, the Cantillon effect, reinforces the development of a two-tier society consisting of a ruling class and a class that is being ruled.

It naturally follows from these observations that civilizations will develop very differently, depending on the quality and type of money that is being used.

Natural money stimulates the building of complex societies based on a high degree of capital creation and voluntary cooperation. They are money that build, distribute wealth broadly, and they strengthen our social bonds.

Political money, on the other hand, stimulates the development of societies of the type that rulers prefer. Because this type of money is a wealth extraction device, it creates societies where a small minority accumulates wealth, while the large majority must work harder and harder to maintain their living standard.

Political money is money that destroys wealth, concentrates wealth in the hands of the few, while it at the same time creates and deepens conflicts between people.

The most important lesson,
however, is that a ruling class who
controls the money supply is able to
win almost every conflict with the
rest of society.

The reason being that the ruling class always can finance suppression with printing more money, while the people must work to obtain the money that they need to finance their resistance.

In such a situation the people will have more than enough just by trying to get by in everyday life, as they won't have any time and energy to spend on politics.

Yuval Harari's understanding of money

The main thesis in Harari's *Sapiens* is that humans are "mythmakers." He goes on to say that it's "shared myths" that allow us to cooperate and organize at scale. Harari argues that understanding humans is about understanding the myths they share.

Already at this stage I find reason to pause.

Isn't the key to understanding human beings that we take a holistic view of what it is that we have in common with other species, and what it is that distinguishes us from them?

For instance, what is it with humankind that makes us create capital together?

Does it have something to do with the extent of our ability to understand the concept of time, and that we are far more advanced in this respect compared with all other species?

What if we try to explore how our use of money relates to the concepts of time preference, meaning how patient we are when it comes to satisfying our needs, and capital formation?

Furthermore, what about taking a deeper look at the phenomenon that Rutger Bregman teaches us in his wonderful book, *Humankind – A Hopeful Story*.

Bregman demonstrates that *Homo sapiens* is different from other species because we have an amazing capability of copying each other's behavior and that, if we are free, we copy good behavior and cooperate instead of copying bad behavior and coerce each other.

Let's leave that aside and go back to the concept of money.

In Sapiens, Harari argues that money is a myth. Is it really?

In all fairness, we should expect that his view of money might change over time. However, when he later wrote the book *Money* in 2018, he just expanded on the same concept. I decided to listen to Lex Friedman's interview with Harari on Friedman's popular podcast.

The episode was released 17 July 2023, and I wanted to check out if his main thesis had changed. In the interview, Harari explained what I expect are his up-to-date ideas about money.

He said:

> "Money is the most successful story ever told, more successful than any religious story."

> "It's just a figment of our imagination."

> "You take these green pieces of paper dollars."

> "They have no value, you can't eat them, you can't drink them. Today most dollars aren't even pieces of paper. They are just electronic information..."

> "We value them for one reason, that we have the best storytellers in the world, the bankers, the finance ministers, these people they are the best storytellers ever."

> "They tell us a story... that this piece of paper is worth a banana."

> "People believe it. It works."

As we see, his view hasn't changed at all. If anything, Harari has doubled down. It's the *mystical* concept of money, that money is a "myth" that only exists as "a figment of our imagination" that sits front and center in his thesis.

When you compare this with my exposition above about how money emerges naturally because of voluntary human interaction and how different types of money produce different societies, you realize that Harari only makes broad dogmatic statements about money.

Harari also argues that it's this "myth" of money which is one of the most important myths that enables us to organize at scale.

I agree that the monetary system is extremely important, just like Rotshchild did. The problem is, however, when Harari doesn't understand what money is and what it does, how can he understand *in which way* money makes us organize society?

Let's dig deeper into Harari's analysis of money, or should we say – the lack of analysis.

You see, his book *Sapiens*:

» doesn't present governments' monopolization of money creation

» doesn't explain that inflation is a policy

» doesn't mention the Cantillon effect

» doesn't make any distinction between political money as a means of wealth extraction and centralization of capital and power on the one hand, and natural money as a tool that facilitates complex societies with strong bonds between people and decentralized wealth on the other.

» and most importantly, Harari doesn't mention that a ruler who controls the money printer is destined to win almost every challenge he is faced with, including from people who feel oppressed.

No other policy has such profound effect on human-kind and civilization as monetary policy. It's the most powerful weapon that a politician can have.

Yet, Harari doesn't mention it in what is supposed to be an introduction to our history. This is nothing but remarkable.

The following is a key quote from his book:

> *Money is the only trust system created by humans that can bridge almost any cultural gap*

Here we see that Harari calls money a "trust system."

But is this really correct?

On the face of it, Harari's description of money as a "trust system" fits with money that is based on debt.

However, this is just one type of money. Debt money requires trust, in the meaning that it must be possible to make the final settlement, that the debtor is able and willing to make the payment.

But commodity money is basically trustless. Commodity money in fact *replaces* the need for trust. It makes it possible for people who don't trust each other to cooperate extensively. And this isn't because we trust the money. It's because we are willing to engage in *the generous tit for tat game*.

We use the money as long as it works, because it's better than reverting to barter or to put an end to interhuman cooperation.

In short, we don't use the money because we trust them, but because the alternative, not using them, is worse.

Let's look closer at this key statement by Harari. We have two types of trust-based money: political debt money and natural debt money. Yes, I am perfectly fine with calling *natural* debt money trust-based.

But what do we find when we analyze *political* debt money?

When it comes to political debt money, it isn't trust, but *coercion* that makes us use them.

The ruler forces us to use his debt money, for instance to pay taxes to the government.

We also see proof of the fact that we don't trust this type of money at all when we observe what happens when someone uses it as payment to ourselves.

When the money is credited our account, most people try to spend them as soon as possible. Instead of saving them, we at once go out and spend them on various consumer goods, in addition to investing in assets like real estate, stock funds, bonds and other securities.

But why are we doing this? Why don't we instead *save* much more of the money, so we can enjoy a more prosperous future?

The main reason is that we know that we can't trust the political debt based money at all.

In fact, we know that they will start betraying us as soon as they appear in our bank accounts.

For instance, the creation of new American dollars (USD) and new Norwegian kroner (NOK) is so rapid, that these currencies halve in value every 10 years.

This is the necessary result of adding on average 7% to the money supply each year. The effect over time is what we call *negative compound interest.*

Most people are unaware of how rapidly our wealth is being extracted away from us, but we understand intuitively or subconsciously that the money loses value fast. Therefore, we try to get rid of them as soon as we have the opportunity and hope that at least some of the things that we buy protect our purchasing power a little longer.

In summary, we use political debt money not because we trust them, but because we are being coerced into using them, and we spend them fast because we know that the money will betray us if we keep them.

In conclusion, it's the very opposite of trust that makes us use political money.

In the quote we also see that Harari says that money has been "created." A natural interpretation of his use of the word "created" implies that he is of the opinion that the myth of the concept of money has been created. And, as you saw, he argued that the bankers and the finance ministers are "the best story-tellers in the world," suggesting that they have been instrumental in the creation of the money myth.

But, as I have shown above, humans haven't created money as a concept. Money was something that emerged naturally over time as we got better at cooperating with each other. It was a social process, which resembles Darwinism in nature.

At some point we *discovered* that some assets had become money. But we didn't *create* them.

Even the various concepts of political money haven't been "created."

Rulers have always used regulation and coercion to make the people use something that resembles various types of money that emerged naturally in society. This doesn't have anything to do with "creation" of a concept.

Harari must by necessity become lost in the jungle of information when he builds on such an analysis, as he tries to develop his understanding of what humans are and how civilization evolved.

When he argues that we in the next phase will become *transhumans* and that he predicts that most people will end up as more or less useless consumers, while a minority elite will become gods, *Homo Deus* as he calls it, we should take it with a grain of salt.

You should notice, however, that such an extreme difference between the ruling class and the rest of the people is the result we get when we let a system based on political debt money continue.

It's also interesting to note how Harari's vision of the two-tier society with consumers and gods fits like a glove with the policy recommendations coming out of the elitist WEF.

It's unfortunate that Harari's analysis misguides intellectuals and others to try to join the elite class that he foresees shall be the one that shapes the course of civilization.

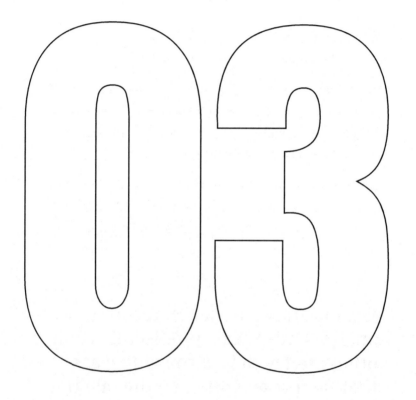

How civilization scales in layer

Today's unipolar order

Today's world order is a hegemony dominated by the US. Simultaneously, we see a rapid decline in citizens' individual freedom, and an increasing level of centralization of power and economic wealth.

Furthermore, we see a seemingly endless string of American foreign military operations. Political activist and author Medea Benjamin commented on this in a powerful article in *The Guardian*. He wrote:

> *President Obama did reduce the number of US soldiers fighting in Afghanistan and Iraq, but he dramatically expanded the air wars and the use of special operations forces around the globe.*

Benjamin then went on and listed the following key facts from Obama's foreign policy in 2016:

» US special operators could be found in 138 countries, representing 70% of the world's nations, 130% more than during the Bush administration.

» US military forces dropped at least 26,171 bombs, an average of 72 bombs per day, and three bombs per hour.

» Most of the attacks took place in Syria and Iraq, but the bombs also rained down on people in Afghanistan, Libya, Yemen, Somalia and Pakistan, in total representing seven Muslim-majority countries.

» Obama used drones outside the declared battlefields of Afghanistan and Iraq, mainly in Pakistan and Yemen.

» He classified all males of military age in these regions as combatants, making them "fair game" for remote controlled killing.

There is reason to believe that this is at least partly caused by a unipolar system, seemingly antithetical to freedom, peace and ethical distribution of wealth.

I share the view of a growing number of activists, communicators and writers who argue that these effects are closely tied to the dominance of the US dollar and the role it plays in dictating global monetary policies.

Focus

Instead of supplying a detailed exposition of the global monetary system and the world order, the rest of chapter 3 focuses on the following question:

What is the belief system and the monetary system that forms the basis for American global hegemony?

Analytical tools

Analysis of the biggest questions concerning the society we live in are often made complex and hard for readers to follow. The reason is partly that writers tend to write out their analysis from a position that's unhelpfully obscured by their own location *within* the system itself.

It can be compared to a situation where you stand in the middle of a dense forest, with trees blocking the view in every direction, making it impossible for you to know the extent of the forest, and what surrounds it.

To deal with this difficulty, I will trace historically relevant social and political developments over time. Understanding and comparing past events makes it easier to analyze current affairs. In essence, it's an exercise where we place ourselves outside the system that we are a part of, akin to climbing a hilltop to get a better overview of the forest that surrounds us.

I also make use of axioms that simplify the analyses. Such tools must be selected carefully. They must be both robust and true, or at the very least, they must represent something that we can say is highly likely to be true.

As an example, my analysis of the social order we call civilization takes as an axiomatic starting point that civilization scales in layers.

Layer zero represents people's belief system.

Layer one is the monetary system.

The other layers of a civilized society build on top of the monetary system.

Partly because you cannot build a civilization without money, I find that these axioms by necessity must be true.

At the same time, we must acknowledge that higher layers also will affect the belief system and the monetary system. Democracy, education, legislation, taxation, socialist policies and innovation in technology are important examples. If they didn't affect the belief system and the monetary system, the latter layers wouldn't change over time, which evidently has happened.

Due to this interplay between the layers, the scaling phenomenon should not be seen as a fixed law. Instead, it is a means to structure the thinking around which factors that have a higher level of importance, and which factors that have a lower level of importance.

Money and civilization

Money has existed as a tool to make it possible for people who don't know each other to cooperate for as long as we have had civilizations. The first civilization that we have significant amounts of knowledge of emerged about 5,000 years ago in Mesopotamia, what is now Iraq.

We have many examples of rulers making laws about which money their subjects had to use depending on which goods or services they bought. History shows that rulers often also tried to regulate prices for goods and services, as well as exchange rates for different types of money.

However, it would take a long time before rulers monopolized the creation of money and used this privilege to inflate the money supply.

When people from different cultures traded with each other they used a myriad of commodity money and commodities as means of exchange.

Inflation policy in Athens

The first historical example of government monopolization and political debasement of money is probably from the Greek city state of Athens, some 2,500 years ago. This implies that monetary freedom, the right to use whichever money you like best, probably had been civilizations' most prevalent monetary system for a good period of at least 2,500 years.

It's not easy to know what part of their belief system that led the rulers of Athens to introduce a new policy. It seems, however, to be the case that the rulers of the ancient city state used the policy of forced coin debasement, and thereby wealth extraction and manipulation of the money supply, to finance imperial ambitions and rule over more people. More specifically, the information we have about such a policy relates it to the rulers' need to cover the costs of the Peloponnesian war against Sparta 431–404 BC.

In the end, Athens lost the war. However, the policy of inflation through debasement of coins started to spread to other areas.

Inflation policy in the Roman Empire

Towards the end of the first century AD, the Roman Empire began debasing its silver coins. This policy fueled the empire's expansion into new areas, but, in the end, inflation also played a crucial part in bringing it to its knees.

The problems eventually led to the dissolution of the Roman Empire as it was split down the middle. The Western Roman Empire collapsed in 476 AD, while the Eastern Roman Empire persisted until 1453 AD.

We don't know for sure which belief system formed the basis for the Roman rulers' choice of monetary system, but once more we see that it's innately linked to war and ambitions to rule others.

Monetary freedom in Norway

My ancestors in Trøndelag, a large region in the middle part of Norway, probably were one of the last peoples of the Western world who enjoyed the principle of monetary freedom. In 1050 AD this window became temporarily closed for the people in the civilized world for about 500 years.

The Trønders used money from many other countries and preferred coins with a high share of silver or gold.

Again, we cannot know for sure which belief system this was based on. What we do know, is that the Trønders were famous for their contempt for kings, and that they had a social and political structure that was highly decentralized.

The Frostating law had "resistance provisions" which basically obliged every Trønder to kill the king if he appropriated anyone's property without the consent of the Frostating, which was the supreme court and assembly of free farmers and landowners in Trøndelag.

If the king didn't adhere to the rule that he needed the consent of the Frostating before he lay claim to somebody's property, it was the duty of every Trønder to pass on a bidding stick to their nearest neighbor. The stick was inscribed with a message that instructed them to immediately meet at a given location. By passing on the stick as quickly as possible this readied the whole society to hunt down the king and his men in the shortest possible time.

If the tyrannical king was left alive, the families and villages could permanently lose their freedom and the protection provided by the law. Choosing not to go after the king was game-theoretically unattractive, and therefore probably not a real choice.

The Norwegian Royal Sagas have preserved a story which illustrates the effectiveness of my ancestors' rule of resistance: In the eighth century AD, the Trønders were invaded by King Øystein of Oppland. He appointed his son as King of Trøndelag and went home. As soon as the Trønders got the opportunity, they killed their new king.

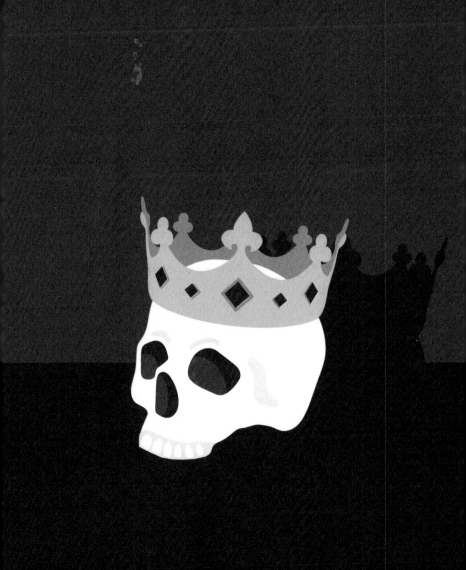

The reason was likely that the resistance provisions still applied, and that the duty to kill the king didn't stop when the war ended.

The resistance provisions ensured three things, that kings had little or no power in Trøndelag, that they had relatively weak incentives to invade the region and that the people would continue to enjoy their freedom.

The long-held principle of monetary freedom finally came to an end in 1050 AD after the ruthless King Harald Hardråde and his men killed Einar Tambarskjelve, a powerful leader in Trøndelag, and his son Eindride. The pretext was that Einar had organized the other landowners in resistance and made them block Hardråde's requests to the Frostating for raising taxes.

The killing of Einar and Eindride was a cowardly plot which took place at the King's estate in Nidaros, the town that today is named Trondheim. Einar's men hesitated for a moment and didn't obey the resistance provisions.

The people of Trøndelag and the rest of Norway were at once punished for their sins, as Hardråde went straight ahead and introduced his inflation policy throughout the kingdom.

Hardråde was ambitious, and he readied the people of Norway for war, having set his sights on conquering England. His reign came to a bloody end in 1066 in the Battle of Stamford Bridge. Hardråde lost the war and was himself killed alongside 4,000 – 6,000 of his own soldiers. The catastrophe also marks the end of the Viking Age.

We see that the monetary freedom in Trøndelag was secured by a simple code of conduct:

Kill any king who doesn't rule by consent.

The inflation policy, by contrast, was based on King Hardråde's personal political ambitions, most fundamentally to wage imperial war and rule as many subjects as possible, including the people of England.

Monetary freedom in the Netherlands

Following the successful rebellion in 1566 against tyrannic inflationist kings and emperors, the Dutch reintroduced the principle of monetary freedom. This meant that the new monetary system was conceived in rebellion against the ruler.

The new policy became the foundation for the so-called Dutch golden age, which lasted until the beginning of the 18th century. An underlying reason was that gold and silver became more valuable in the Netherlands versus in the rest of Europe due to the other countries' inflationist rulers. This led to a massive inflow of capital, investors and entrepreneurs into the small country.

Over the course of this period, the Netherlands became a globally leading trading nation and one of the richest countries in the world.

The original traces of monetary freedom in their own history may have been wiped out before the Dutch rebelled against their rulers. The rebels were inspired by monetary freedom traditions that could be traced back to the 8th century AD in a part of India that was ruled by Muslims.

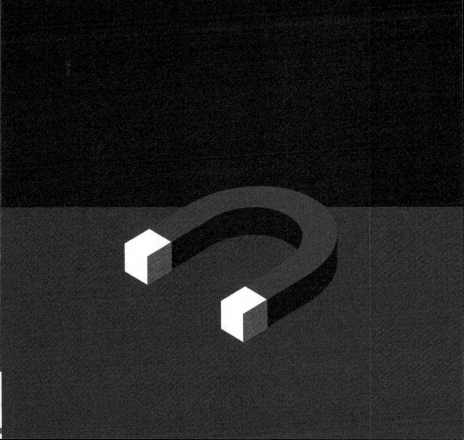

These traditions had spread to parts of Portugal and finally to Portuguese colonies that later became part of the Dutch colonies.

You should note that Harari, who writes extensively about the Dutch golden age in *Sapien*, doesn't mention monetary freedom at all or how this turned the small country into a powerful capital magnet.

Instead, Harari explains the success with the country's massive use of credit. If Harari had taken a look at how the Bank of Amsterdam operated in one of history's most impressive tales of growth, he would have seen that finance was based on sound, full reserve banking. Starting in 1657, the bank succumbed to the temptation of letting customers overdraft their accounts. This became a turning point, as the Dutch society later experienced an explosive growth in credit – and which in the end smashed the golden age to pieces.

In conclusion, what Harari has interpreted as the recipe for success, was in fact the recipe for disaster. This is what may happen, if you try to interpret history without understanding money and economics.

Monetary freedom in the US

The people of the US had de facto monetary freedom after the revolution, which started in 1775 and ended in 1783, and well into the 19th century.

This meant that, once more, the new monetary system was conceived in rebellion against the ruler.

The principle was indirectly protected by the new republic's Constitution and the Bill of Rights. This included the right for everybody to bear arms. The objective was that everybody should have the possibility to defend themselves against oppressive rulers. The embodiment of these essential human rights in the constitution guaranteed an extremely high degree of individual sovereignty and that the state would have very limited power over the people.

It was also probably of great help that several of the Founding Fathers believed inflation was a crime against humanity. Some of them went on to become political leaders of the new government, securing a continuation of individual freedom and resistance against an intrusive state, and helping this ideology become a key part of the American society's belief system.

When you're rarely forced to interact with the government or its agencies, perhaps except for the occasional visit to the post office, people will tend to be relatively flexible when it comes to which money they use.

They will prefer coins with a high and dependable share of valuable metals, with a design that enables recognition and which are known to have a stable value.

For these reasons, the Spanish silver dollar served as the unofficial national currency in America for much of the 17th and 18th centuries. The foreign coins even became legal tender, a status which was preserved until the Coinage Act of 1857.

In addition, local and regional banks issued different types of paper currencies which were used as money in what was called "the free banking era."

Just as had previously happened in the Netherlands, the US experienced a massive influx of industrious people and capital, especially from Europe. There can be little doubt that the de facto monetary freedom contributed greatly to the US growing into an economic powerhouse.

Monetary freedom is put to sleep

The revival of the principle of monetary freedom that started in the Netherlands in the 16th century, and which continued in the US, lasted for about three hundred years.

From a policy-development point of view, it was the combination of a 200-year long experiment with central banking in Europe and the introduction of the gold standard across almost the entire world in the 1870s that eventually undermined the system.

When the Federal Reserve, the first real central bank in the US, was sanctioned by law in Congress in 1913, and World War I broke out in Europe in 1914, the principle of monetary freedom was effectively put to sleep.

Since then, the entire world has lived under largely the same type of globally coordinated inflation policy, first dictated by the British and the Americans, and later by the Americans alone.

Preliminary summary

As we see, monetary freedom has grown out of people's general desire of freedom and the acknowledgement of the simple fact that if you want to retain your freedom, you are obliged to fight to protect it and rebel if it's lost. We may call it the Code of Resistance.

On the other hand, the policy of inflation goes hand in hand with war, imperial ambitions and suppression of individual freedom. This is what we may call the Code of Coercion.

These two very distinct monetary systems and the underlying codes on which they are based, emanate from two opposing belief systems – the love of individual sovereignty and freedom, and the idea that you must be subservient to the state.

The Code of
Resistance

vs.

The Code of
Coercion

Our contemporary monetary system and how it supports the current world order

The specific geopolitical system we have today is layered upon a specific monetary system, which in turn is layered upon a specific belief system.

Our current geopolitical order is what Obama, Biden, Merkel, Macron, Stoltenberg and other globalists often have referred to as "the rules-based order." This is in essence a system of American hegemony where the US dictates the rules that the rest of the world must follow.

The unipolar system depends on the monetary system that we basically can call "the dollar standard."

In practice, this system implies that the US and its closest allies, which are mainly the English-speaking countries, the EU and Norway, inflate their currencies in tandem and in a controlled manner, meaning at a tempo that isn't too high relative to the rest of the world. At the same time, they actively encourage the rest of the world to take out loans denominated in USD.

By being careful not to create too much inflation, this arrangement enables dominant countries to have relatively strong currencies.

The combination of the policy and the military supremacy of the US enables the American political elite to force its inflation upon the rest of the world.

As a result, their most valuable export commodity has since the end of World War II been the US dollar, which the Federal Reserve and private banks "print out of thin air."

In return, the rest of the world exports commodities and various other goods and services at artificially low prices back to the US.

The Euro area countries to some extent enjoy the same benefit through the euro, which is the second biggest currency in the world.

Furthermore, the French government controls the CFA Franc, a currency which is legal tender in fourteen poor countries in West and Central Africa, twelve of which are former French colonies. The French use this arrangement to exploit the labor of approximately 155 million Africans and to extract commodities, such as rare minerals from their land.

The conflict in the ultra-poor country of Niger is probably related to people there being tired of being dominated by the French.

During the summer of 2023, the military rebelled against a president who had been supported by the French government.

These events created a tense geopolitical situation as France lost access to the cheap uranium that it had used as fuel in its production of nuclear power. The former colonial power also risked that the rebellion could spread to the other CFA countries. At the time of writing, the situation is still unstable.

The rest of the worlds' governments also enjoy the benefits of inflation, but their policies are more concentrated. With the implicit or explicit consent of the US and the EU, they debase their currencies at a higher speed.

The reason why I used the term "artificially low prices" above, is that countries that create money at a high tempo destroy their domestic capital structure and extract tremendous amounts of wealth from their own people. When their citizens are kept poor, these countries can produce products and services at lower costs compared to the developed countries.

A share of the fruits of the poor people's labor is also typically directed into state coffers controlled by corrupt and tyrannic rulers supported by the Western countries, as well as into the pockets of the "client" countries' wealthy elites.

If we simplify our analysis, **the global dollar standard** can be defined as an arrangement that effectively is a symbiosis between

a) the US government and its ability to exploit its own citizens and the rest of the world by exporting its inflation, and

b) the ability of governments in other countries to exploit their own people by debasing their own national currencies that tend not to be used beyond the borders of their states.

A key outcome has been that, except for a handful of nations in Asia, developing countries have been unable to accumulate capital and industrialize. Instead, they continue to be comparatively poor commodity producers who send cheap goods to the developed countries. Alex Gladstein's new book *Hidden Repression: How the IMF and World Bank Sell Exploitation as Development* has been instrumental in uncovering that this system is a de facto continuation of colonialism.

The American people and those who live in other developed countries enjoy *a net benefit* from the dollar system, because their governments have created a monetary system that extracts wealth from the developing world. However, it is very important to understand that developed countries experience a severe redistribution of wealth within their own society.

In the US, the policy is typically beneficial for those who are in high-tech, entertainment, the industrial-military complex, media, education, pharmaceuticals, public utilities and bureaucracies and other sectors that the government prioritizes.

The redistribution is fatal for people living in areas such as the US "rust belt," where skilled workers continuously are laid off as manufacturing companies move their operations overseas.

It doesn't take a genius to understand that the global monetary system therefore enables governments to capture and control the private industry, and to quickly make them subservient to the state, just like the citizens.

The belief system on which our current monetary system is layered upon

The next question we need to ask is which belief system the global dollar standard is layered upon. In order to answer that, let us first focus on the birth of this monetary system.

The Age of the Dollar was conceived in the biggest war that civilization has ever experienced – **World War II**

When the *Bretton Woods conference* took place in July 1944, it was relatively clear already that the allied forces would win, but that this outcome depended on the continued support of the US.

The forty-four allied states who attended the conference set up an international quasi gold standard with the dollar as the circulating currency, backed by reserves of gold. In practice it meant that the Americans could inflate its currency beyond its gold holdings, merely using the gold as a fractional reserve.

In turn, the other countries could inflate their own currencies, using their dollar holdings as their own fractional reserve.

All the countries, including the Soviet Union, agreed on these principles and signed the treaty.

I would argue that the belief system underpinning this decision, that is, of the attending countries' rulers, likely was primarily fear. If they didn't support the proposal, the US could threaten that they would contribute less to the war effort, which would mean that the war likely would last longer and shift more of the social and economic cost to the Americans' allies.

But secondly, the proposal served their own greed and ambition, because in reality it didn't leave much of a restraint on their ability to extract wealth from their own citizens via the inflation policy.

What happened next was that the US delivered on their promise to end the war with an Allied victory. However, they did much more than that.

When American airplanes dropped nuclear bombs on Hiroshima and Nagasaki in August 1945, the US administration headed by President Harry S. Truman also demonstrated an unprecedented ruthlessness and an unmatched technological ability of destruction. This contributed greatly to peoples' fear of the new super-power and a possibly devastating nuclear war.

It can be no doubt that this extreme level of aggression made it easier for all the parties to the Bretton Woods agreement – with one important exception – to ratify the treaty. On the 27 December 1945, the agreed-upon threshold of signatories was met, and the establish-ment of the quasi gold standard was a fact.

After the dollar system was conceived in war and cemented through final acts of immense terror, it would survive for a long time on greed and fear. Let us now examine the fear component.

The Soviet Union abstained from ratifying the Bretton Woods agreement, as the communists argued that the Wall Street banks were the ones in control of the new monetary system. This went hand in hand with Stalin´s ambitions to further the idea of international communism.

The combined effects of the cold war and the many proxy wars between the two post-World War II super-powers, meant that the Western countries and their aligned third-party countries solidified their support of the dollar-based monetary system.

Thus, fear of global nuclear war and feeling of being dependent on US military protection against the Soviet Union was the belief system that the quasi gold standard was layered upon.

After president Richard Nixon in 1971 announced that the US would not deliver on its promise to exchange gold for dollar, the same belief system continued to underpin the new, slightly modified global monetary system. The US government managed to secure its currency's status, by promising military protection in exchange for Saudi Arabia and other nations supporting the dollar by accepting it as payment in international trade, primarily oil.

When the Soviet Union and the East Bloc countries imploded in 1991, the neocons took the conscious decision to give financial support to some countries, such as Poland, while leaving Russia in the cold.

The consequence was that hyperinflation broke out in Russia. This sparked political turmoil, paving the way for a weak oligarchical political system that would cripple the Russian bear for years to come.

Shortly before the collapse of the Soviet Union, President George Bush Sr had established close ties to Chairman Deng Xiaoping. The arrangement the US and Chinese government put in place in the beginning of the 1990s basically implied that the Russians should be marginalized on the global stage, and that China should be brought into the fold of the dollar-based global monetary system.

This would be achieved by the Chinese accepting USD as payment for consumer goods and buy US treasuries with the surplus USD that they would amass. In exchange, the US would open its vast consumer market to exports of cheap Chinese goods.

The flipside of what later has been dubbed the "Chinese Miracle" was that many Americans slowly were turned into unproductive consumers, having deindustrialized their domestic economy and destroyed their own export potential. As China built financial institutions and allowed the accumulation of capital and industrial know-how, the giant in the east would gradually come to outcompete the Americans' once dominant manufacturing industry.

Another notable consequence would be that the arrangement made it possible both for the Chinese and the US government to take out large and comparatively cheap public loans backed by future tax income, effectively printing huge sums of money. As a result, both nations now have become heavily indebted.

It can be argued that the belief system that the dollar system was layered upon during the last 32 years to a large extent was consumerism and the idea that one could pass on the bill to the future generations of taxpayers.

The dollar standard has also been kept alive by numerous military interventions in countries that tried to opt out of the dollar, American-led economic sanctions and regime change operations. Lyn Alden, who recently launched her bestselling book *Broken Money*, is one of several analysts who argue that these interventions form a pattern that is consistent with such a motive.

The US-led wars against Iraq, after Saddam Hussein started to sell oil for euro, and Libya, after Muammar Gaddafi launched his plans to sell oil for gold, seem to be two of the clearest examples of this policy.

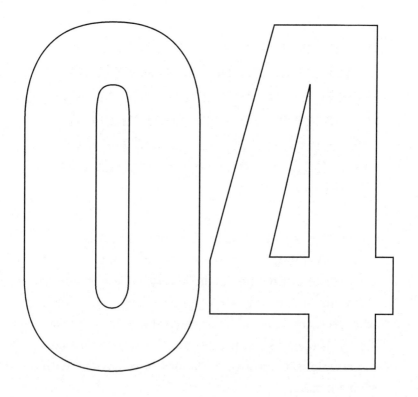

Risk factors for the dollar system and the American hegemony

Under pressure

In recent years, the US government and the dollar standard has come under increasing pressure. In the following I'll discuss seven of the key developments that threaten the current world order.

Weaponizing the dollar becomes increasingly difficult

The ability of the US government to weaponize the dollar has already been diminished through the large-scale deindustrialization and, therefore, a lower manufacturing capacity than the superpower needs to continue to wage wars to support the dollar's dominance.

The news that broke in the summer of 2023 that both the US and the other NATO countries were running out of conventional ammunition shows the graveness of the problem. In what on the face of it looks like an act of desperation, Biden's administration, as reported by *Politico.com* on 6 September 2023, decided to ship ammunition with depleted uranium to Ukraine.

Unsustainable public debt levels

US public debt currently sits at about 33 T (trillion) USD corresponding to a whopping 120% of GDP. Reaching these levels has been made possible thanks to the Federal Reserve and other central banks gobbling up US treasuries in the secondary market. The various central banks have made a consorted effort to print money out of thin air to make this happen.

Alden and other leading analysts argue that the debt level is unsustainable. They also argue that it's mathematically impossible to avoid a further expansion of the debt levels, since it is simultaneously politically untenable for the government to end all the programs financed in part by printing money.

The debt constitutes in itself what we may call a threat of internal economic implosion, which is the same fate that the Roman Empire, the Soviet Union and the East Bloc countries eventually all succumbed to.

Furthermore, the high level of debt also means that creditor nations increase their political leverage, thus reducing the US governments possibility to dictate what other countries can and cannot do.

The BRICS nations want out of the dollar

The original BRICS bloc consisted of Brazil, Russia, India, China and South Africa. In April 2023, their combined GDP for the first time topped that of the G7 member states, which consists of Canada, France, Germany, Italy, Japan, the UK and the US.

After the 15th BRICS meeting, which took place in August 2023, the bloc now also includes **Saudi Arabia, United Arab Emirates, Iran, Egypt, Ethiopia and Argentina**. This makes it a group with significant economic and political influence.

One of the organization's top priorities is to reduce the members' use of USD in cross-border payments and to create an infrastructure that facilitates increased use of their own currencies. The idea seems to be that they want to build an infrastructure that replaces the SWIFT system, which is an outdated, five decades old international messaging system for payments built around the dollar standard.

The dollar is still dominant as a global reserve currency, but its share has been steadily declining from about 70% to 60% since the turn of the millennium.

In August 2023, even the US Treasury Secretary Janet Yellen had to admit that the dollar's share of global reserves may continue to decline as countries look to "diversify."

The high value of the USD is partially a result of its salability, meaning, it's high share of payments in global trade. Over time, the reduced use of the USD has a negative impact on its value.

The plans of the BRICS-11 to further reduce the dollar dominance therefore represents an organized threat on a global level against the dollar dominance and the rules-based order.

Creditor nations increasingly favor gold over US treasuries

The US government finances its deficit spending by borrowing money. It auctions off various debt instruments, or IOUs, to the highest bidders. The result of the auctions decides the interest it must pay. High demand gives low interest rates. Low demand gives high interest rates.

Investors' demand for IOUs with relatively long maturity, US treasuries, used to be high. This meant that the US government got cheap loans.

Treasuries can easily be exchanged for USD and vice versa in the financial market. As a result, treasuries are "as good as money," something which improves the salability of the USD. Therefore, the demand for treasuries is of the utmost importance for the value of the USD.

Lately, two of the major countries that invest in treasuries, Japan and China, have reduced their buying. On 16 August 2023 *South China Morning Post* reported that:

> *China cuts US Treasury holdings to 14-year low amid persisting security concerns, geopolitical tensions.*

In consequence, fewer players want to lend money to the US government. It becomes more expensive for the government to borrow money, further deepening its problems with the high debt level.

Gold is the main competitor to treasuries. It's a very rare and sought after metal. All of the gold that has been mined throughout history would fit into two Olympic-size swimming pools. Miners are historically only able to increase the total global amount of gold by less than 2% per year.

The total value of all the gold in the world, which we refer to as gold's market capitalization, is currently about 12 T USD. This makes it the single most valuable global asset.

In comparison, the total value of all USD in circulation is currently about 20 Trillion USD (broad money M2).

Gold continues to play a role as a store of value, for the general public, investors and especially for central banks. For the latter, owning gold might contribute to a more stable and a stronger national currency.

While the BRICS and other nations have reduced their buying of treasuries lately, they have instead quadrupled their gold holdings since the Great Financial Crisis of 2008.

In stark contrast to the BRICS, the Western allies of the US have been reducing their gold holdings in the same period. Interestingly enough, the central banks of Canada, New Zealand and Norway have sold out all of their gold.

Nobody knows how much gold the US Federal Reserve holds, as it keeps a tight lid on this information.

If it comes out that the United States' share of global gold holding has declined, this will most likely have a negative impact on the value of the USD.

Bitcoin has rapidly manifested itself as a real threat to the USD.

It took only 12 years from Bitcoin emerged in 2009 until its total market capitalization reached 1 trillion US dollars.

This made Bitcoin the fastest growing asset **ever.**

Although the price plunged in 2022, the market cap today sits at about 500 B (billion) USD. Bitcoin is still one of the global top-10 money, also when we include gold.

It should be noted that the Bitcoin network, which is completely decentralized and controlled by no single entity or groups of entities, has become the safest and most powerful computational network in the world.

Furthermore, it's the fastest global payment network in terms of transaction speed and final settlement. These features make Bitcoin become a threat to the clunky SWIFT infrastructure.

Bitcoin is also on its way to becoming the backbone of the next generation's payments services. By adding so-called "sidechains" and "layer two" systems, such as *Liquid* and *Lightning*, the network can facilitate transactions of other types of money, including national currencies and cryptocurrencies, at near instant speeds.

When we look at the Bitcoin technology, its emerging ecosystem and the rapid adoption rate, we must expect that it facilitates de-dollarization and reintroduction of the principle of monetary freedom.

The BRICS-11 might look at using the trustless Bitcoin network as backbone for cross-border trade with their own currencies. The alternative, to build a competing and trust-based infrastructure will be costly and, due to the political complexities, we should expect that it will take a long time before it's ready for implementation. This presents a dilemma for the BRICS-11, as they presumably would avoid strengthening Bitcoin which slowly undermines their own ability to print money out of thin air.

In conclusion, Bitcoin represents a threat because it's an innovative and completely decentralized monetary and payment technology that is almost impossible to stop.

Political polarization within the United States

There is an increasing degree of polarization inside the US federal republic, as the disagreement between Democrat voters and Republican voters seems to grow by the day.

The fact that only 4% of Democrats are married to Republicans perfectly illustrates the deep divide between the American people.

Some of the states dominated by the Republicans have decided that gold and silver are legal tender, support Bitcoin mining and block the central bank's plans of introducing a Central Bank Digital Currency (CBDC).

It seems to be the opposite with states dominated by the Democrats, which align themselves with the Biden administration's policies.

This happens at the same time as people are beginning to realize who it is that has benefitted from the money printing over the last few years. As entrepreneur and analyst Balaji Srinivasan has pointed out, it has shifted a notable share of the Americans' total wealth from Republicans to Democrats.

Srinivasan cleverly also points out that the end game might be a race towards the republic's exit door, as states dominated by Republicans realize that those who choose to remain in the republic might have to carry the whole burden of the country's public debt. He points to the fact that this was what happened when the Baltic states successfully were the first to break out of the Soviet Union.

One important factor seems to be that most of the administrations in the US after the collapse of the Soviet Union, perhaps with the exception of President Donald J. Trump's administration, have pushed the US further and further away from a policy which supports the country's hegemonic status. In hindsight we see that much of its own policies has undermined the uni-polar order, and moved it towards a system that global elites, not the US, will be in control of.

The Biden administration's policies increasingly seem to be aligned with the ambitions of the UN and the WEF. The closest allies of the US have moved in the same direction, with the EU, Canada and Norway rapidly becoming extreme examples of such a development.

At the same time, Biden's support seems to unravel, both among his voters as well as among political leaders in the allied countries. It's getting impossible to ignore his deteriorating health and reduced capacity.

The average Democrat voter probably also watches with disbelief the consequences of Biden's open border policy, as hundreds of thousands of illegal immigrants cross the border every month and flood the streets of New York and other cities.

The backlash might become intense, as ordinary Americans' support for the Republican party and especially for former president Trump seems to be on the rise.

Ironically enough it therefore seems to be the US itself, greatly helped by Biden's administration, that destroys the fundamentals for the country's own hegemonic status.

In conclusion, political polarization constitutes an increasingly grave threat of internal political implosion in the US. This weakens the superpower, but whether it plays it into the hands of the globalists or if it makes the world pivot back to a more multipolar world order remains to be seen.

Knowledge about the evils of political monopolization of money spreads fast

In general, theories of money and inflation haven't been taught in schools. Even students of economics and finance at university level learn next to nothing about the monetary system, while the history of monetary policy is largely ignored in the curriculum. The general knowledge level surrounding monetary politics has therefore until recently been very low.

People in the so-called "goldbug" community understand monetary policy and quite a few of them seem to argue for the reintroduction of a gold standard. Their views have gotten limited traction among economists. One of the reasons is that most economists have been trained within the traditions of economic schools who support and subsist on political money.

When US Congressman Ron Paul from the state of Texas ran for president in the primary elections in 2008 and 2012, he conveyed the message of the importance of sound money and taught Americans about the role that gold has played in our civilization. This contributed greatly to a popular revival of the ideas of freedom and sound monetary policy.

Outside the US, the general public seems to be oblivious to the goldbugs' efforts to promote an alternative monetary policy.

However, the distribution of knowledge about money and the effects of inflation as a policy can spread very rapidly in the Internet age. After Bitcoin's inception in 2009, the Bitcoin community has grown into an impressively forceful movement in terms of pushing the debate on monetary policy. One can argue that it has become a much-needed continuation of what Ron Paul's movement started.

It's likely that no other community has ever taught so many so much and so quickly about the evils of inflation and manipulation of the money supply as the Bitcoin crowd has managed to do.

The principle of monetary freedom is rarely mentioned when goldbugs and Bitcoiners discuss monetary policy. The debate between the two groups easily becomes centered around the question of which type of money that is best, gold or Bitcoin. However, we now see anecdotal evidence of some degree of convergence between them, as goldbugs begin to dip their toes into Bitcoin and vice versa. This seems to be a natural phenomenon since they share a common understanding of the problems with political money.

The rapid distribution of knowledge is a decentralized threat against the US hegemony that is impossible to stop and it acts as a catalyst for the other pressure mechanisms described above.

The continued dispersion of the age-old wisdom about the evils of the inflation policy and the effect this has on shaping people's belief system might be one of the reasons why the US government, the EU and their allies now spend so much political capital in a move towards limiting free speech.

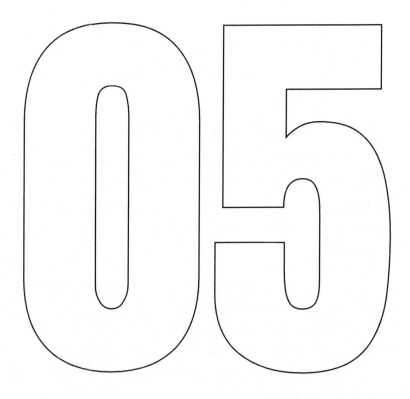

SUMMARY AND CONCLUSION

Decision time

I will now summarize some of the key points that we have looked at, give you a final analysis and offer my conclusion.

In the introduction I asked you to find your inner rebel. UNBAR has showed you why that is important. Let me just say, that I'm a firm believer in non-violent revolution, and that I'm not going to ask you to do stupid or illegal things. However, we are quickly approaching crunch time, and the question is if you want to join me in the fight to win the battle of the ideas.

Others have done things before us that greatly improved our freedom and without using any weapons. For instance, when the Wright brothers defied the elite scientists' ideas, they became the rebels who revolutionized the way we travel the world.

In comparison, our task is a walk in the park. We are just going to show the rest of the world that we have rediscovered a lost wisdom – the fundamental importance of the right to use the money we like best, and that we want it back.

The reward, on the other hand, will be much greater.

The monetary system

Chapter two gave you the most important lessons:

Firstly, that having a monopoly on money creation is the most powerful weapon that has ever existed.

And secondly, that the government and the super wealthy use it continuously to accumulate power and wealth and to finance everything they need to hold the people's resistance at a manageable level.

You also learned that we have two types of natural money, commodity money and debt money, that they emerged in society in a Darwinian-like way. These types of money strengthen our ability to succeed when we play the generous tit for tat game.

This is the great enabler for capital formation and development of an advanced civilization with decentralization of wealth and where people form strong bonds.

Furthermore, UNBAR has explained how political money affects society negatively, as it supports centralization of power and wealth and the development of two distinct classes, a small ruling elite that lives off the creation of new money out of nothingness, and a large majority of serfs who must work harder and harder to earn the counterfeited money to maintain their living standards.

This part of UNBAR also showed that Yuval Harari is right when he concludes that money is a foundational factor for humankind's ability to cooperate and scale.

However, as we saw, we have ample reason to disagree with his presentation of money.

Harari makes people believe that they can never really understand money, because it's just a mystical concept that only exists in their imagination and that they just have to trust that money works, because trust is the only reason why it has ever worked.

He has made maximum use of the quasi-philosophical concept that we call "deconstructionism," as he has reduced money to something that only exists as "figments in our imagination," to use his own words.

In my opinion this is nothing but cheap, *new age* storytelling. The problem is that it has worked wonders as a way of hypnotizing lazy intellectuals. Harari amplifies the confusion of people who feel confident because they have spent so many years in schools and universities, but who never have been taught how different forms of money affect the development of civilization.

It's ironic that many of them now want to become members of an elite group tasked with guiding the rest of us while they create a new world order where they themselves become our overlords.

Instead of continuing to be hypnotized by the ideas of Harari and his ambitious friends in WEF, they should make good use of whatever capability they have left for independent and critical thinking and question their own belief system.

How civilization scales in layers

In the third chapter we had a look at *how* civilization scales in layers.

The people's belief system is layer zero, while the monetary system is layer one, as it's built upon the people's belief system. The rest of the civilization, including its laws, is layered upon the monetary system.

We saw that the system we call monetary freedom has grown out of people's general desire of freedom and the acknowledgement of the simple fact that if you want to keep your freedom, you are obliged to fight for it.

We also saw that the policy of inflation goes hand in hand with war, imperial ambitions and suppression of individual freedom. It can be summarized as the Code of Resistance vs. the Code of Coercion.

Furthermore, we concluded that these principles emanate from two opposing belief systems – the love of individual sovereignty and freedom, and the idea that you must be subservient to the state.

As we traced the development of monetary freedom and inflation policy, we dived into how the current dollar system was conceived in war and maintained on the basis of weaponization of the dollar, interventionism, creation of fear, consumerism and passing on the bill to the younger generations.

We saw that the unipolar world order is primarily maintained by a powerful symbiosis between the US government and its ability to exploit both its citizens and the rest of the world, by exporting its inflation, and the ability of governments in other countries to exploit their own people by debasing their own national currencies that tend not to be used beyond the borders of their states.

Frictions in today's world order

In the fourth chapter I discussed how the American hegemony is shaken due to a number of pressure mechanisms:

1. Weaponizing the dollar is becoming increasingly difficult

2. Unsustainable public debt levels

3. The BRICS nations want out of the dollar

4. Creditor nations increasingly favor gold over US treasuries

5. Bitcoin has rapidly manifested itself as a real threat to the USD

6. Political polarization within the US

7. Knowledge about the evils of inflation spreads fast

People's understanding of the monetary system and how it affects our lives and society is an "X factor" of unknown significance, especially because it acts as a catalyst on the other factor.

The people's most effective weapon

When you have read UNBAR, you have hopefully understood that a ruler who has a monopoly on money creation has a weapon that makes it *possible* for him to win every battle.

But you have probably also realized that he will not be able to win *every* battle. Civilization isn't a finite game, with a given start and a given end. On the contrary, it is a *process* where battles are lost and won and in which the people's belief system can have a significant effect on the outcome.

It's my conviction that it once again will be the belief system that decides which monetary system and global order we will have to live with in the near future.

The combination of **knowledge and sound money** is our best weapon.

There is no stronger social force than the network effect we create when we **share** knowledge and sound money with people that we love.

If the distribution of knowledge of the importance of reforming the monetary system shall get any traction, we need to acknowledge that we only have two alternatives – monetary freedom, or rulers having a monopoly on creating money out of nothing.

I cannot emphasize strongly enough how important it is that goldbugs and Bitcoiners converge on this worldview.

The alternative, to stay divided and let one specific form of money, gold or Bitcoin, be their religion, will in my opinion only help the globalists to move forward with their plans.

Looking forward

If I managed to prime your brain into becoming receptive to these ideas and that you were able to read the full text without being thrown into fits, I'm happy for you.

Hopefully UNBAR has made you appreciate that it was people who loved individual sovereignty and freedom who kept the principle of monetary freedom alive, and that it was the rebels who rediscovered its importance and restored it as the civilization's cornerstone.

All I hope for now is that you make sure to pass on the bidding stick to your neighbor.

If you do, we can destroy the ruler's weapon and set ourselves free.

Afterword to the youth

You may have heard people say that "the youth is our future."

This is only true in the sense that a system based on political money depends on the next generation to volunteer and become part of it.

Don't make that mistake.

Especially, you must be careful and avoid borrowing money. If you do that, you plug yourself into a system that allows a small elite to feast on you.

The correct phrase is "the youth owns the future."

Let it sink in: You own the future!

It's yours.

The Wright brothers gave you an immensely valuable gift – the possibility to fly.

Now, find the freest parts of the world, order your ticket and go there.

Our creator gave you the ability to learn languages. Make use of it.

Nature gave you natural money. Freedom loving people developed Bitcoin. Learn how to verify, earn and save sound money.

Remember that freedom, responsibility and resistance are inseparable values.

Leapfrog my generation by using AI to rapidly develop skills that we spent years in school to get.

Practice the generous tit for tat game until you become experts.

Let others copy your good behavior and learn from your insights.

Leave the mess that earlier generations have created. It's our responsibility to clean it up.

And if you want to, come back and visit us when we have updated our software.

– Rune

Acknowledgements

Reading books and articles by Friedrich A. Hayek, Ayn Rand, Robert O. Paxton, Murray Rothbard, Ron Paul, Saifedean Ammous, Jeff Booth, Alex Gladstein and Lyn Alden, and listening to them and other great thinkers and communicators of today, such as Balaji Srinivasan, Peter St. Onge, Glenn Diesen, Michael Saylor, Nic Bhatia, Lawrence Leppard, James Lavish, Greg Foss, Max Keiser and many others on platforms such as What Bitcoin Did, The "What Is Money?" Show, TFTC, the Bitcoin Standard, the Simply Bitcoin, the Swan Signal and the Duran Report, have been great sources of knowledge and inspiration.

Apart from the perspectives on the importance of the generous tit for tat game in the development of civilization and natural money, the analysis of monetary freedom, and the idea that monetary freedom should be at the center stage in the policy discussion, UNBAR is mainly a synthetization and systematization of other people's ideas and insights. However, I don't claim to be alone about these ideas, as I expect that others have expressed the same without me being aware of it.

Mattis and I would also like to give a big thanks to J.K. Baltzersen, Hodlonaut, Jens Emil Asp, Christopher Bendiksen and Gregard Mikkelborg for proofreading and tips.

If there are any errors in the book, it is solely my responsibility.

– *Rune*

Follow us

You find both of us on *X* and *Nostr*

Rune Østgård @enur72
Mattis Storhaug @mrpixelparanoia

Visit **undoqo.com** and stay up to date on our projects.

Bibliography

For bibliography, please see undoqo.com/pages/unbar

Printed in Great Britain
by Amazon